Data Analytics

Essentials to master Data Analytics and get your business to the next level

Table of Contents

Introduction-

The information in the world doubles every 12 months. Important data sources are business and industrial processes, text and structured databases, images and videos, and physical and biomedical data. Data analytics allows finding relevant information, structures, and patterns, to gain new insights, to identify causes and effects, to predict future developments, or to suggest optimal decisions. We need models and algorithms to collect, preprocess, analyze, and evaluate data, from various fields such as statistics, machine learning, pattern recognition, system theory, operations research, or artificial intelligence. With this book, you will learn about the most important methods and algorithms for data analytics. You will be able to choose appropriate methods for specific tasks and apply these in your own data analytics projects. You will understand the basic concepts of the growing field of data analytics, which will allow you to keep pace and to actively contribute to the advancement of the field.

Chapter 1- Introduction to (Big) Data Analytics

What is Big Data? Big Data is any voluminous or big amount of Unstructured, Structured and Semi-Structured data for which you can get information's or can be "mined" for individual purposes. We call it "Big Data" when normal data becomes difficult to process using normal or traditional techniques.

Let talk about characteristics of Big data:

1. Volatility: It's related to how long will take for data to be valid since that data which is valid at this moment will not be valid anymore after a couple of moments. That change could easily take place in a matter of minutes or hours or days.
2. Variety: It's related to the type of formats that are being used and can be classified into 3 big types:

First one Unstructured: Here we talk about photos, videos, audio files and text files(short text files).

Second one Semi-structured: When it comes to Semi-Structured data we are talking about e-mails(that can by categorized by data when they have been sent, subject, receiver and so on), Tweets(by hashtags) and Log files

Third one Structured: Here we talk about MySQL, we talk about Excel documents, Access documents or anything that can be organized and measured in a way or another.

3. Volume: It's related to big data volume, that implies volume of data generated by machines, computers, storage devices, e-commerce, social media and so on.
4. Velocity: It's related to the rate that that is pouring like in social media platforms where users generate big amounts of likes comments, tweets, follows and so on per day.

The importance of Big Data

Due to the fact that big data it's being used in organizations, corporations, big and small business also, the success of an organization lies also in how good and effective an organization analyze their data and also get their insights correctly about their company activity and competitors. We are in the era where data(or Big Data) can make the difference between success or failure by taking the right decision at the right time. As a matter of fact, you can know pretty precise who is your competition and how big your competition is. Data it's being delivered through different channels and different sources that nowadays are being available to the normal person. Things are getting reduced on getting DATA to have what to analyze and also to

UNDERSTAND how to analyze it. "Knowledge it's potential power if it's not being used" it doesn't help you at all just to have data if you can't read it.

Data Analytics have their own terminology. Understanding terminology its part of the process. This is a field where constantly new and different terms appear and are being thrown around by everyone. The are a LOT of terms that have similar attributes and instead of helping you are just creating more confusion around the subject that it's being talked. They may sound different and effective to use but can be easily interchangeable and be new to Data analytics can very easy create a lot of confusion and even be pretty intimidated by the abundance of terms that will make this domain to appear more complicated and harder than it is.

Analysis of data, also known as data analytics is the process of inspecting, transforming and modeling data with the specific goal of discovering specific and useful information supporting decision-making. In other words, it's the process of taking a specific problem and breaking it down into smaller pieces and looking for simple parts that can be used for taking decisions.

Analysis of data is not a specific tool, rather a way of thinking and putting everything together. Business analysis has his specific application in the sphere of business, marketing analysis has his specific application in the sphere of marketing. Here we can talk about Marketing Analytics, Risk Analytics, Fraud Analytics, CRM Analytics. Data preparation and data exploration is an essential part of our process and analysis relies on that and on descriptive analytics. Big data Analytics is a new expression used to describe the Analyze of unstructured data.

For Big Data Analytics we use "material" terabytes and petabytes of data (a not normal type of data, can't be stored by individuals, requires servers and special storage equipment and also special tools for analyze).

Classification of different type of analytics

Analytics can be used to a lot of problems and also can be applied in many different industries and that transform analytics in something very powerful and important to take in consideration.

Classification of different type of analytics can be made by three big and broad criteria's:

1. Based on the industry that data it's coming from
2. Based on the business function and requirements asked
3. Based on the kind of the insights offered

Based on the industry data it's coming from let's start looking to where data analytics usage is very prevalent. There always have been industries that produce a big amount of data that required to be analyzed. Consumer good and financial information's for example. Those type of industries were in the first lines when it came to adopting analytics. It's generally classified in the industry and how it's applied hence you encounter terms like insurance analytics, web analytics and so on.

When it comes to a data set users have a different point of interest for what they will be looking for. Take a look at the following classification for the "task" and the general description given for a better understanding.

1. Task: Retrieve Value

   General description: Given a set of specific cases, find attributes of those cases

   Example: How big it's that artist discography?

2. Task: Filter

   General description: Given some conditions on attribute values, find data cases satisfying those conditions

   Example: What team have won the championship?

3. Task: Range

   General description: Given a set of data cases find the span of values within the set

   Example: What is the range of film lengths?

4. Task: Sort

   General description: Given a set of data cases rank them according to some ordinal metrics

   Example: Order the cereals by weight per package.

5. Task: Distribution

General description: Given a set of data cases and a quantitative attribute of interest, characterize the distribution of that attribute's value over the set

Example: What is the distribution of macronutrients in your diet?

Classification of analytics is based on the basis of business functions that is being made by the following:

- Marketing analytics
- Sales Analytics
- Supply Analytics

Descriptive analysis is the simplest type of analytics that can be used to perform those type of analysis. One of the reasons that it's so simple it's that uses information's from the past to understand present decisions and if they are correct to help to make future decisions/predictions.

Due to the fact that it's pretty easy to understand the application of descriptive analytics this often can be considered subdued analytics.

In general, retailers pay a closer attention in understanding the relationship between products. Retailers usually are looking to see if a person that buys a specific type of product will buy something complementary to that product and how they can link more and more products to the base product.

Predictive analytics work by identifying patterns and historical data and also use statistical information's to make predictions about future sales, future requests of the clients and so on.

Lifecycle of data analytics

Analysis of data or data analytics as any measured information has a lifecycle. You can't use the same type of data over and over because will lose validity and reliability. Data can be used over a period of time, let's take for example sales information's related to Christmas sales, from the first of December to the last that of the year will have a specific validity. You can't relate to those information's that you are receiving from your data analytics all year around. In December you will have usually a big spike in sales and in January and February you can easily aspect a little drop in sales due to the fact that people usually start the year with new resolutions, new plans, and goals. So lifecycle of data analytics it's a VERY important aspect to take in consideration when dealing with big amounts of data to analyze. Let's consider the following stages or steps of a data analytics project lifecycle:

- Correct problem identification
- Creating and formulating a hypothesis
- Creating a process of data collection
- Starting data exploration
- Starting data preparation
- Validation of the model that has been created
- Evaluation of the results

A correct problem identification is the first step in any analysis you start doing. Without a correct problem identification, you will not get the most accurate information's possible. You can find yourself start doing an analysis of a problem without having the RIGHT situation in place you will get results , after which you will model your business. If the information's you are getting are not guiding you in the right direction may cost your business, be careful.

A problem's something that it's being perceived as something that needs to be corrected. In that situation, it's your responsibility to solve it and to get the right processes in place.

The problems that we encounter in the business world are pretty straight forward, sometimes easy to resolve sometimes more difficult than we can image. We meet with situations where we have to reply on questions like:

- How do I monetize my business right now?
- What is the best way to convert my audience without losing them?
- How do I optimize my costs by maintaining the same quality of your services?
- How do I detect capital glitches in my business and how do I correct them?
- What resources do I need to produce the result I want?

   This one I consider to be the most important question in my opinion .

In my opinion getting the problem clear it's the most important thing for avoiding confusion around what you have to do. Spending time on establishing the right questions it's valuable. Get the right question and you will get the right answers.

Let's take for example a situation in a design/ web development company. If you have experience and knowledge in the field of design/ web development. If you have a problem identifying clients that pay on time and clients that don't pay on time and determining the clients that don't pay on time to send you the checks. Out of your database, you will have to gather information's about those customers and send them private messages to see what was the channel the acquisition for that type of client, if there exists a pattern for that type of client and so on. The list can continue to question related to that subject by the main idea has been explained. Identify the situation and then ask the correct questions in order to get the right answers. Basically the relationship it's backward, starting from the final phase to the first phase.

The example above was a simple situation that can be very easy resolved and documented because of the fact that you have a lot of data in your company files.

On the other side developing a face recognition algorithm will imply more than the situation above and the complexity of the questions will be bigger and obviously the efforts for answering to those question.

Getting a clear vision about your problem sometimes can be more difficult than discovering the answers to your questions. I advise you to start with a conceptual definition and look for the root cause, impact of the situation etc. A problem becomes visible when it's being identified the difference made in the actual situation and favorable situation. Identification can be made by using:

- SWOT Analysis – taking a view on strengths, weaknesses, opportunities and threats
- Surveys results – online /offline audience answers
- Performance results – getting information's about the current performance compared with your goals
- Checklists with targets achieved

We often take in consideration situations that are not real problems, but due to the unclear vision, we make them appear even as a priority in the analysis that we are doing in problem identification. If we would take into consideration a situation like the following: customers are refunding in a proportion of 15% more than they used for last two months we definitely can say that we identified a situation/ a problem and the "Why" question is what will help us to discover the root of the problem:

- Why are customers are not satisfied?

- Why are customers not satisfied in last 2 months?

- Why are customers not satisfied in last 2 months taking in consideration that the product has not changed at all?

Part of the question that can be asked to go slowly to the root of the problem and basically make a data analysis backward. This is just a side of the problem. In the way, you are doing the analysis for identifying the root you have to identify HOW to FIX the situation. It's not enough just to understand what caused the problem. Finding a way to discover the solution or what may be the solution it's as important as the first questions we asked:

- What can be done now that we know what is the problem?

- How much will cost us to fix the problem?

- What are the resources that we need in order to remediate the damage?

- How long will take to get the sales back where they were?

Creating and formulating a hypothesis

Formulate a hypothesis now. Break down the problem and get down also the hypotheses. Having the hypotheses down will help you to get the right question as we talked above, the topics of interest and finally the path to solving the problem.

- Build your path to success. It's a matter of getting down the pieces of the puzzle
- Develop a list of possible problems that you need to take in consideration when developing your hypothesis
- Reduce all the useless information's to the lowest possible, you need to focus just on essential

Creating a process of data collection

At this point usually you come pretty far away, usually, at this point, you will answer or have answered to some very important questions that you formulated earlier and you are just validating the hypotheses created. At this point please keep in my mind that is very important to use different techniques for your data collection. Data collection it's critical in problem-solving if it's being made in a superficial way or not done data analysis will be very difficult to complete.

Techniques of data collection:

Offline Methods:

- Verbal questioning of people, either individually or as a group
- Collect data by written surveys or written opinions
- Creating or facilitating free discussions on the topics that you are interested in a group of people that will help you to get the type of data you are interested

Online Methods:

- Create a survey using Google Forms or any other platform for creating surveys
- Create a Facebook group where you can add people to collaborate on the specific topic and consult them for information's
- Create a landing page to get people's e-mail address in order to create a database of random people to see different opinions on the subject you are interested in.

Start data exploration

As a data analyst or future data analyst before a data analysis can be realized you should start by knowing how many cases are right now in the dataset, also what variables and type of variables are included and after that how many missing observations are and the general hypotheses set of data you have it's possible to support.

Start data preparation

Usually, when you got here you have data collected you explored the dataset and the variable available and unavailable, you have created hypotheses and pretty much every step that it's required it's covered. Working with data usually, it's not easy because data comes in a very alembicated form. When data preparation it's being made, a data check and after that, a data refresh needs to be made. A check for consistency also its required in order to start to analyze.

A couple of data preparation steps and methods that can help you:

- Get the data imported into the software you are using for analysis. Usually the format it's a very general format like .xls or .xlsx in case you work with Microsoft Excel documents or the specific format that your software uses
- Check for variables and variable identification. If it's the case then create new variables for your analysis
- Check and summarize the data
- Combine data from different sources if needed in order to prepare it
- Treat outliers that are being identified in your dataset. Outliers are values that are not respecting a pattern, usually, are not giving the most accurate information.
- Select subsets of the data

Variable identification: Identification of the input and the output variables and also the date type in the dataset you are working with is very important. Create categories for your variables by using a frequency table to get a better understanding of each category.

Validation of the model that has been created

To validate your model you must realize that are many variables before decision taking from a business perspective. Analytics being one of the most common ways. Obviously, there are more ways to take decisions, not just this one, go by your "gut" but this one won't assure you that you are really taking the best decision even though not every time when you are taking a decision you will have an analytical approach.

Fundamentally if you want and need data to decision making I strongly advise you to be sure that you have invested enough in collecting the right data.

Evaluation of the results

This is a continuous process, that is essentially aiming to look after effective solutions over time. Remember that this approach is orientated on problem-solving in an analytical way.

This is different from that standard problem-solving a way to resolve a problem. Key points to have in mind:

- The analytical techniques that we using right now are based on numeric theories
- A good understanding of theoretical concepts will build a feasible solution

You need to have a great understanding of the situation that you are dealing with in order to have the right analytic approach. In some industries, your solutions may last 2-3 years till you need to refresh it and at little tweaks here and there to it. Also as time goes by you will have to check for dependability over time and also for any changes that may appear.

Frequent mistakes: The client usually causes all the mistakes and he is usually the person that makes the situation harder to resolve. Due to the fact that the client usually lacks in knowledge and experience(no reason to judge for that), he usually has difficulties formulating the right problem. Without a concrete problem its hard to create the solution for it, in special when you are working with numeric theories and concepts. Be cautious about recommendations that you are making to your client, check for his understanding, most explanations require some degree of investment in coaching the client to understand the situation.

As we talked in the previous chapter Data Analytics is depending a lot of statistics. We have to use the science of statistics for classifications, analysis, and interpretations.

A business man usually encounters problems like the following that need a statistical approach in order to solve them:

1. How to reduce operational costs of the business? A problem that every entrepreneur faces when starts his business

2. How to develop a successful relationship with your client and also what is the best channel to use in order to do that? Your client's not your enemy it's your ally. Serve your client with respect and he will also treat you with respect by appreciating your products and as a natural consequence acquiring long-term customers that will keep your sales high

3. Should I invest more in the online or offline side of the business? Due to the fact that online commerce it's developing crazy in last years, it's something that you really want to take in consideration. Having an online presence will just help to pump your sales and get even closer to your client. Nowadays, everybody, it's online. On

a personal computer, tablet or mobile phone(in most cases) everybody it's firstly checking online and then for offline product or service.

4. What is the right inventory to start with on each product and with how many products start with right now? Offline businesses often encounter these situations, not knowing how much inventory to take when they are just starting. The online side of the business can definitely give a help by the different KPI (key performance indicators) that are being integrated into the platforms we use.

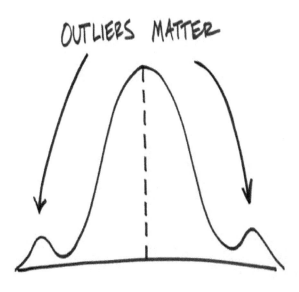

Statistical terms

In order to create a good data analysis using statistical tools and information's, we have to get used to the statistical terms. So let's take a look at main statistical terms that is very probable to met in your projects or scenarios:

- Sample is a subset (a smaller piece) of the population that is being selected for analysis
- Population is representing the total set of components or items used that share a common characteristic
- Statistics is a measure that is calculated on the sample
- Descriptive Statistics are being used for both describing and summering data in ways that are relevant and useful. We can describe data like a general tendency, a measure of distribution and measure of dispersion.
- Predictive Statistics are representing methods with are being used to predict future probabilities based on historical data
- Inferential Statistics are representing methods for deducing the properties of a population from the data analysis
- Random Variables: a random variable is a variable whose value is representing the subject to variation caused by change.
- Variables: Variables are representing a characteristic very important in statistical science. Variables can be measured and counted.

    Data can be classified into the following 2 types:

1. Quantitative Data: is representing a measured type of data, usually expressed in numbers.
2. Qualitative Data: this type of data is data that can be set into any number of groups or entities. Without having an ordering we call those nominal variables and is we have an ordering we call those ordinal variables.

Different scales of measurement

1. Ratio Scale: this type of scale is a scale that satisfies a number of four types of scales of measurement like intervals, identity, magnitude and absolute zero.
2. Nominal Scale: this one is a scale that is focused on satisfying the property of measurement. For a better understanding, we can take as an example the gender of an individual, we classify by giving values as "male" or "female".
3. Ordinal Scale: this scale is more focused on magnitude when it comes to measurement. On an ordinal scale, each value has his unique identity. Let's take for example numbers from 1 to 5. 1, 2, 3, 4, 5 each number has a different value and of course a different identity. Another example can be evaluation by quality: bad, average, good, very good, excellent
4. Interval Scale: the last scale that we take for an example is the interval scale that has magnitude and identification characteristics. A perfect example for this situation can easily be Fahrenheit scale or Celsius scale for temperature measurement. Those scales of

measurement are giving you an interval of temperature for this to this, from the lowest temperature to the highest temperature.

Techniques for sampling

Sampling is a technique often used in statistical science. Sampling is used to draw a sample from the population. We can talk about different sampling techniques. Samples are used to estimate population parameters or any other characteristic.

Selecting the Sampling Frame: Sampling frame is representing just a list of items or information's which creates a sample

Typical downsides in sampling:

- Data from volunteers can be inaccurate taking in consideration surveys, Facebook groups, online reviews, and the list can go on and on.
- Picking easy respondents can be difficult
- You can get a high rate of non-responder depending on the audience that you are making the survey, for example, CEO or CFO of companies

Let's talk about probability

When we are dealing with uncertain situations, like we find in business it's pretty important to have an evaluation for the situation, what is the risk and what we have to take in consideration in making a decision related to that. Any decision that we take in our life either it's related to business or not has a chance of not putting back the outcome that we desire, by other's words, we "failed" or we didn't succeed in our attempt. When it comes to probability analysis we will have to look first at the following conditions:

1. The number of events that may occur(one, two or more depending on the situation that is being approached)
2. Where can occur the events that we are talking about

Let's talk about random variables

We approach random variables because they describe the best the probability of an event that has no contain future outcome(numerical outcome or measured outcome). Variables take in general several positions and are random because there can be a chance to associate each a possible value.

Chapter 3- Machine Learning explained

During our life, people have developed lots and lots of systems to help us improve our work and also our life. From simple mechanism, we went to more complex mechanism and systems till we finally developed "Machines" that can make our life simple and more efficient. Machines are designed to organize our work and give us some help, to help you work more consistently and more efficient. Have you ever thought of the fact that machines can learn also? Have you ever thought about that? Or how machines can help us automate more and more tasks, either if we are talking about business tasks or day to day tasks.

Let's think about a couple of things that we can ask you about machines:

- What is the purpose of making a machine learn our behavior or focus on "machine learning"?
- How can we develop that more and more to a higher level?
- How can we assign tasks to machines and what tasks are appropriate to improve machine learning?
- How can we relate the learning to intelligence(or even artificial intelligence) and how can we as humans

develop such extraordinary systems? Keeping in mind that intelligent can't be specific defined or measured

- Can we create beliefs or implant beliefs into a machine or alter a machine learning process?
- Can we create intelligence, we as superior creatures?

Those all are representing a question that we can formulate about machine learning, a subject that I consider to be very important when talking about data analysis or analysis of data. Interpretation of data it's just the next step in our work and machine learning can be part of that interpretation process due to the period of time that we are living in right now.

Data and learning may appear as two different subjects and in a way or another a little bit unrelated. Actually, when talking about data analysis, learning, data mining, interpretation are all related. Life itself can be described as a continues learning curve by receiving lots and lots of data, analyzing it, mining through information's and projecting our interpretations on the situations we deal with under the form of actions. Action can take a different form, action can have the form of entertaining a thought, feeling a specific emotion or going in a specific place. Approaching data and machine learning with an attitude of correlation between them will help you to get a better understanding.

The philosophy of learning it's a subject that has been talked and it's talked because of the importance and how anchored it's in our life. We learn by different methods and we learn with a lot of purposes. Listen to an audiobook, read a book, watch a video(nowadays with access to websites like YouTube video content it's being facilitated more than ever), spend time with a person than can give you valuable information's or maybe try to experiment something different. Learning to play guitar or a new skill if not practiced will be forgotten, we have to apply or better say constant apply on the information's that we are assimilating.

The best combination is to have both practical and also theoretical information. Once we are done with applying and adapting we can say that we have improved our process of data analysis and learning and by the end of this book I'm pretty sure that you will have improved a lot your way of seeing business problems (or life problems) and solutions to them.

Knowledge, a powerful word. In the machine, learning knowledge hasn't the same representation as in human learning. For humans, knowledge and information's have just potential power or relevance if it's not being used, as we talked earlier, without being used it will be lost and will not represent anything practical.

I consider relevant in creating a great product three characteristics based on what we talked till now. Looking for example at CD Player, a great product when it first came on the market, served well for the purpose was created, but by today standards and requirements not any use. The first characteristic that I consider relevant in product creation I consider to be the Interface of the product. Basically the interface it's part of a system that facilities the communication with the used. By today's standards the use and interface of a CD Player it's outdated due to the fact we listen to music on our smartphones or any other device on which we can play music. The interface of the product makes the product also easy to use. No wonder that you see a 10 years old boy setting up a Xbox console in a couple of minutes and just like that he starts playing or even an "old" person being able to configure a device due to the simplicity of the interface.

Another characteristic that I consider relevant in creating a product I consider to be Infrastructure of the product. When we are designing a product we must keep in mind the will not serve just for personal purposes but for a large mass of people. Your focus must be other's experience not just you experience when designing a product, let your attachment to the product itself. The problem of infrastructure it's something will be always present either if we are talking about designing infrastructure of a physical product or digital product. Giving a couple of examples to make everything clear we can talk here about the infrastructure of an operating system like Windows or a digital product like Microsoft Office. Also, we can talk about products used across the globe, for example, social media platforms like Facebook, Twitter, Instagram built a strong infrastructure behind. Also, we can talk about the infrastructure of a building or organization we are talking on the tangible side and how important it is infrastructure for a system resistance.

The third characteristic that I consider to be relevant in product creation is a characteristic that I consider to describe the utility of the product and the "intuition" of the product, Smartness. Let's say for example the auto-suggestion from Google search bar. When you are starting to type a word Google will complete that word for you based on the most popular searches that have been made recently, creating you a better experience as a user. The fact that you have a storage space for your phone in your luggage somewhere very accessible it's something that can be considered smart. Smartness can be anything that in a way or another can be revolutionary (like Apple's products, Google, Internet revolution) not just a big scale but also on a small scale, like a wireless charger, anything that can bring a benefit that will bring a smile on your face meets that requirements. People won't look, won't analysis and not even buy a product that it differentiates itself just a little to the rest of products. As sales person usually say, "it stands out", "lights out" "shines" by how innovative, easy or pleasant it is to use it. I consider this to be the first characteristic of developing artificial intelligence, an important aspect in improving machine learning or anything that is related to the experience of learning.

The time has come!

Data analysis is just the foundation stone for machine learning. Data analysis it's the starting point for everything that comes like data mining, big data analytics, machine learning.

Why machine learning it's so important and why it's important to pay attention to machine learning? Let's talk a little bit about ranking a web page on the internet. The process's pretty simple, you to create a website to submit your website to Google, a search engine and start optimizing your website for searches. To rank your website the search engine, in this case, Google, you must know or "understand" how to rank and which pages are relevant for Google. When it comes to Big Data we can take for example Tweeter where almost 200 million tweets take place on a daily basis. All that data has to be recorded and analyzed in a way or another. Think about Facebook, they have to process over 200-300 terabytes of data every day(pictures, videos, text). Google processes over 10 petabytes of data on daily basis, that type of data have to be recorded and analyzed. Interpretation of data from big amounts of data is what helps the big corporations to improve their services and to serve their customers better and better. An excel spreadsheet will not be enough for you to track all your data, that is sure.

After getting records, statistics come in place, we use statistics to generate pie charts, histograms. Statistical side of the things it's very important for a correct interpretation of the information.

How machine learning really works?

It's not that complicated to understand how machine learning really works. To understand it you will have to think about the nature of the mind and how you get new information's into your mind. What is learning? What is thinking?

One of the goals that a machine has when it comes to learning is to get a derived decision from data. Look at your company and see how your decisions are looking like? Are your decisions being made by your gut feeling or are being made by complex analysis on the information's that you are getting from your clients.

Types of machine learning

There are a couple of machine learning types that we can approach and discuss. Let's take them one by one for a simple analysis.

1. Active learning: this type of learning it's a type of learning that is a teaching method that strives to more directly involves students in the learning process at that moment. It's a learning process that directly aims to involve the person in the process.

2. Supervised Learning: Imagine that your child has just got back from school, is home he has a strong desire to play with yours. He wants to make a drawing. You are giving him a task like: go and draw a car and a house looking like X house(example) and then announce me when it's ready. When you are going to give him that task he is going to research for the task in case he is not documented on that topic, he will have to make a plan and then to execute it. This is called supervised learning. In this type of learning, you will have to label data and to try to find structures (that matches) and also variables by building different models and try different combinations of models till you find the right one.

3. Semi-Supervised learning: this is the third type of learning that we are taking in consideration. For example, let's say that you been given a big amount of labeled and unlabeled data. Semi-supervised learning is supposed to help you to help you with unsupervised learning to combine the data that is labeled to build or create an improved model than the previous one.

4. Unsupervised Learning: the fourth type of learning that is being approached, it unsupervised learning. Let's say you received a lot of data but at the same, you not been told what to look for in that data. You have been given also some papers and some instruments to write and all you have to do right now is to organize information's and sort that out. Basically what I'm saying is to give a sense to that data that you have right there. Be creative and draw something original or write something original, life itself can be compared with unsupervised learning due to the fact that everything we need it's already out there in the nature and now we are just putting everything together when we are making a discovery and we are thinking that we are "discovering" something revolutionary but we are just sorting and giving an order to data that It's already present. In unsupervised learning what we are working on is Unlabeled data.

5. Reinforcement learning: The last but not the least type of learning that we have to take a look its reinforcement learning. This is pretty simple because we are not creating something from 0, we are building a system that maps the whole sequence of actions into a specific outcome. Reinforcement learning is more concerned with how software agents ought to take action in an environment let's say so as to maximize some notion of cumulative reward.

Chapter 4- Business Intelligence in the Era of Big Data and cognitive Business

Doesn't really matter how you call it, business intelligence, data mining, big data, cognitive business, it's not really important the name that you are giving to it, it's important to have in mind that the challenges for realizing a valuable business are the same: Helping business managers and high-level executives to understand what is really relevant for creating value in their business.

Get a refresh on terminology

Even when talking with high-level executives, managers and analysts I realize that a lot of people even people in C suit don't know the terminology right so let's talk a little about the most important ones:

- Business intelligence (BI) – is representing mostly a set of processes, strategies, applications, basically, an umbrella term that its includes everything from relevant reports, scorecards, e-mail alerts and the list can go on and on.
- Big Data: Here we are talking about big amounts of data generated on a daily basis consisting of pictures, video

clips, text messages, documents, web logs mostly found on social media and internet-based businesses.

- Analytics: A subset of business intelligence, a term used to include relevant statistical analyses, forecasts, models, simulations for increasing revenues, reducing costs on business etc.

- Big data analytics is the process of collecting and organizing large sets of data. Here we talk about the analysis of stored big data content from various sources to improve BI traditional analytics.

- Unstructured data: Here we have digital content. Pictures, videos, and text are considered unstructured data

- Structured data: Structured data is used to describe numerical values or information that can be measured, usually the output it's ordinal.

- Data warehouse: this term is describing a database that is being used to store the most important business information's like information's about customers, information's about products

It's about the HYPE

In every day, managers and executives at major companies are just bombarded with claims about BI, data analytics and so on. People in leading positions need to have a concrete idea about what is and how BI, data analytics or cognitive business works.

"The next big thing" in BI comes faster that we think, the change is here, facts:

- Many big companies that have success haven't leveraged data yet.
- Generally, the most valuable data that stand for BI and data analytics are common, customer data, financial data. Data is key for understanding the economic performance of the company
- Big data in natural form is representing unstructured digital content that we talked above(pictures, video clips)
- Many companies don't generate unstructured digital content by normal course in their business

The business view of big data

It's pretty clear that we need to have a business view on big data. From a business perspective, it's important to see what's important about big data. When it comes to big data we can also talk about how big data holds a lot of characteristics like volume, like variety and velocity. Let's have a little look on a couple of characteristics that are specific to big data.

Data volume: when it comes to the internet we can say for sure that social media has made a revolution in how we perceive internet and internet activity and is no argument or negative argument about that. We have spawned vast amounts of new kinds of data during last 5, 10 years. New technical approaches to storing and managing have appeared during this time to be able to keep up with these vast volumes of new data that are being produced. So the result of this is the fact that we had to adapt and to create solutions to store big data cheaply. Having a business perspective in mind is important because we need to know to determine the utility of big data and also the value that big data is creating in business.

Data velocity: We can take as an example of the change in velocity of data the electric utility industry and it's adoption by new technology to improve consumption and the way electric energy it's being produced.

Data variety: Kinds and kinds of data are available nowadays and different ways to measure it. What is supposedly new with big data is the capture and storage of unstructured data or semi-structured data, all of it digital but much of it not really "data" in the traditional sense of the word. Based on what we discussed till now would be good to conclude that the volume and the velocity of digital content creation are needed. Content is king nowadays, "content" or "digital content" (making that distinction between types of content due to the environment) and content has to come in new varieties all the time and bigger and bigger quantities. When it comes to the importance of big data we can easily look up for some reasonable points to discuss:

- New varieties : this I consider to be a very important point when discussing about importance of big data because digital content when It comes in multiple varieties of consumption like (blog article, podcast, YouTube video, Facebook post) can easily increase revenues, reduces business costs due to the fact that you can often take a piece of existing content and recycle it and give to you customer more ways to consume it. Also none the less this will depend on a lot of the industry that you are in right now or the audience that you are targeting. If your target audience consumes content just written or just audio content will be absolutely useless to produce in a form that will now be consumed.

- Increased volumes of content: increased volume of digital content it's more about quantity, putting out the quantity of content in short period of times so you could keep your audience or clients in case you start converting your audience. This is very important because helps you to increase revenue and reduce also costs otherwise you could be spending money on less efficient methods and not that effective.
- Bigger velocities: well-increased velocities of digital content will help you, it's no doubt about that.

The difference between BI and Analytics

Before start talking about the difference between business intelligence and analytics, for learning purposes let me remind before, that when we are talking about business analytics we talk about data-based applications of quantitative analysis methods that are being used in businesses for decades and decades. If you are going to start an extensive research on that you will find out that there are a dozen books or maybe hundreds of books that apply various quantitative analysis and even discrete mathematics method to specific business domains that are ranging from complex client segmentations and predictions to customer simple client segmentations and optimization requests. Earlier we defined pretty broadly business intelligence as un umbrella term that encompasses the provision of relevant and important reports, dashboards, analyses, forecast and so on. The most common business intelligence applications that provide analytical perspectives include the following characteristics:

- Reports: we talk about standard reports, advanced reports and performance based reports
- Scorecards & Dashboards: as the names says we talk about convenient forms of multidimensional analyses that are pretty common and usual across organizations, scorecards and dashboards let you to rapid create an evaluation of business trends, events evaluation or performance results. That makes possible the use of a common management framework.
- Multidimensional analyses: are related to applications that have the purpose of leveraging a database of trusted business information
- Advanced analytics: advanced analytics usually are applications that can be automated or require little effort to obtain a result that extracts historical information's related to business.
- Predictive analytics: predictive analytics are applications that mostly have the purpose of leveraging descriptive statistics and business information's and stated business assumptions.

How industry sees Business intelligence

The whole purpose of business intelligence use is to provide value to managers and people in leading positions like executive and directors. This is the main objective of business intelligence to offer value, knowledge, and analyses that can create positive business results. What results you get as being relevant in your domain may not be relevant in another domain. Keep in mind that the results that you are getting are not recyclable, so you can't guide yourself that indicators of profitability or customers preferences when it comes to a type of food may be the same after one or two years. Business intelligence for an inventory analysis is crucial for a company expansion. Due to the fact that business intelligence uses are pretty extensive, business intelligence success looks different depending on your company point of interest.

For companies in manufacture industry BI success, it's based on having the ability to manage and improve performance in the most important departments of the company that has the biggest impact towards the customer.

Conclusion-

That being said those are the essentials of data analytics and how they can improve your business and make everything easier for you.

Thank you again for downloading this book!

I hope this book was able to help you to understand how body language affects us and also enjoyed the book!

The next step is to be sure that you fully understand the information, also apply it and read it as frequently as necessary.

Finally, if you enjoyed this book, then I'd like to ask you for a favor, would you be kind enough to leave a review for this book on Amazon? It'd be greatly appreciated!

If you enjoyed this book check out other releases that you might like:

Passive Income: 3 Proven Business Models That Generate Online Revenue to Achieve Financial Freedom

www.ingramcontent.com/pod-product-compliance
Lightning Source LLC
Chambersburg PA
CBHW070902070326
40690CB00009B/1965